MW01233227

THIS JOURNAL BELONGS TO:

Charlotte Ragsdale

ISBN: 979-8-9855922-3-8
Published by CMD Publishing

CMD PUBLISHING

www.camridorsey.com

POSITIVE PERSPECTIVE JOURNAL

Hi! I'm Penelope.
Congratulations on choosing to have a positive perspective on life! A positive perspective is about making a choice and taking control of your own inner voice.

In this journal, you will find prompts to practice your positivity and doodle pages with positive affirmations. Share your thoughts with pictures, words, or both! To learn more about changing your mindset find me in my book, Penelope's Perspective.

A positive perspective can change the way you see, so the world becomes a more beautiful place to be. What does a positive perspective mean to you?

Fill your heart with positivity! Draw what makes you happy in each heart.

I AM LOVED.

Imagine your perfect day.
What does it look like?

TODAY
IS THE
Perfect
DAY

I AM IN CHARGE OF MY LIFE.

Breathe in positivity, breathe out negativity. Using figure 8 breathing, trace the shape and practice controlling your breath.

I CHOOSE CALM.

There are so many amazing people in our lives. Who is someone that you are thankful for?

Thank you

I AM GRATEFUL.

Life is like a puzzle, it's the little pieces that make the big picture. What are four important pieces of your life?

MY LIFE IS BEAUTIFUL.

Smiling increases positivity!
How can you make someone smile?

I CARE ABOUT OTHERS.

Help change them change their perspective from negative to positive.

> I got a C on my homework. I'm always going to be bad at math.

STOP AND THINK, "HOW CAN I SEE THIS DIFFERENTLY?"

I CAN DO HARD THINGS.

Things can always change for the better! What was a time when a situation seemed bad but turned out okay in the end?

MY CHALLENGES HELP ME GROW!

Gratitude is the best attitude.
What are you thankful for?

I AM THANKFUL FOR...

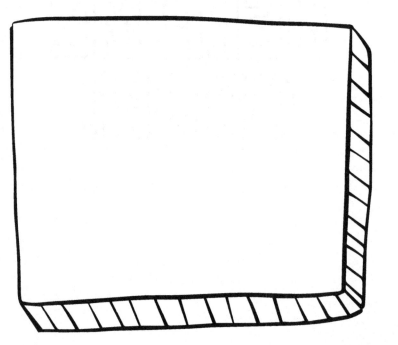

I AM THANKFUL FOR EVERYTHING I HAVE.

It feels good to be around positive people. Who is the most positive person you know?

STAY
Positive

I AM AN AMAZING PERSON.

The power of yet makes everything possible. Those 3 little letters will make you unstoppable.

What is something you can't do... YET!

I AM DETERMINED.

Feel your feelings.
How are you feeling today?

I AM COURAGEOUS.

Good ideas need to be shared!
What is an idea that you have?

I WILL DO GREAT THINGS.

We rise by lifting up others. What would you do to cheer up someone you care about?

I AM A GOOD FRIEND.

What is your favorite color?
What can you draw with it?

THIS COLOR MAKES ME HAPPY!

SOMETHING I CAN DRAW WITH MY

FAVORITE COLOR IS...

I AM
IMPORTANT.

The world is full of fantastic places. What place makes you happiest?

I AM HAPPY.

We want to be around positive people! What can you look for in a positive person?

THIS IS WHAT A POSITIVE PERSON MIGHT SAY!

THIS IS WHAT A POSITIVE PERSON MIGHT DO!

I AM BEAUTIFUL INSIDE AND OUT.

Surround yourself with good people.
Who do you like being with?

I SURROUND MYSELF WITH LOVE.

Everyone has a favorite thing to eat.
What food puts you in a good mood.

I THINK HAPPY THOUGHTS.

There are so many wonderful things about you! What is your favorite thing about yourself?

I AM PROUD OF MYSELF.

Mindfulness is learning to be present and enjoying the moment. What are some ways that you can practice mindfulness?

MY DREAMS ARE COMING TRUE.

The way to happiness is overcoming sadness. If you are feeling sad, what makes you feel better?

I WILL ALWAYS DO MY BEST.

Help change them change their perspective from negative to positive.

Everyone has better shoes than I do.

STOP AND THINK, "HOW CAN I SEE THIS DIFFERENTLY?"

I AM ENOUGH.

So many things can bring us joy!
What is something that always puts
you in a good mood?

------------------------ today

------------------------ I CHOOSE

------------------------ joy

MY FUTURE IS BRIGHT.

Spreading kindness spreads smiles!
What is a random act of kindness you
can do for a stranger?

MY RANDOM ACT OF KINDNESS

I AM GENEROUS.

Kindness is a gift everyone can give. What is something kind you can do for others?

I HAVE A KIND HEART.

When we're practicing positivity we need a calm mind. Zig Zag breathing can help! Trace the shape with your fingers as you breathe.

BREATHE IN
POSITIVITY

BREATE IN
BREATHE OUT
BREATE IN
BREATHE OUT

BREATHE OUT
NEGATIVITY

I AM
CAPABLE.

Scary things are out there, but we can always face our fears. What is something that scares you? How can you face it?

I AM
RESILIENT.

Help change them change their
perspective from negative to positive.

We're having carrots for
dinner. I hate carrots.

STOP AND THINK, "HOW CAN I SEE
THIS DIFFERENTLY?"

I TRY NEW THINGS.

Laughter improves your mood!
What makes you laugh?

I AM JOYFUL.

Every part of you has a purpose. What part of you do you love and what is it's purpose?

I LOVE MY _____

IT HELPS ME ...

MY BODY IS ONE OF A KIND.

Every person is born with a talent. What is a talent that you have?

I CAN DO ANYTHING!

Our sense of smell is one of the strongest. What scent brings you positive feelings?

A GOOD SMELL IS A GOOD MOOD.

I LOVE MYSELF.

Love yourself and be proud of
everything you do. What is something
about you that you are proud of?

I'M Proud OF YOU

I WILL SOAR TO GREAT HEIGHTS.

Engaging in our interests can bring us joy. What is something that you like to learn about?

I WAS BORN TO LEARN.

Be yourself, there is no one better!
Describe yourself in at least 3 positive
words!

-------------------------------- *you are*
                                   · ★ the ★·
--------------------------------   **BEST**

NO ONE ELSE IS QUITE LIKE ME.

We usually celebrate holidays and special events. What ordinary act do you think deserves a celebration?

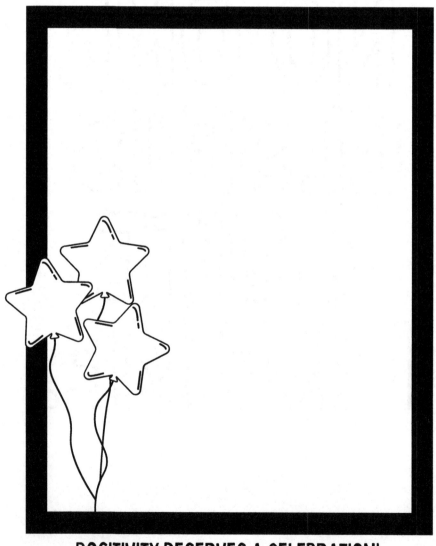

POSITIVITY DESERVES A CELEBRATION!

I CELEBRATE MYSELF.

Dream big and set goals. What is a goal that you have? How are you going to reach it?

I GET BETTER EVERYDAY.

Don't forget to spread positivity online! What would your positive post look like?

I AM
FRIENDLY.

There are many beautiful reasons to be happy. List at least 5 things that make you happy.

I AM WORTHY.

Write a letter to yourself. Tell yourself how wonderful you are!

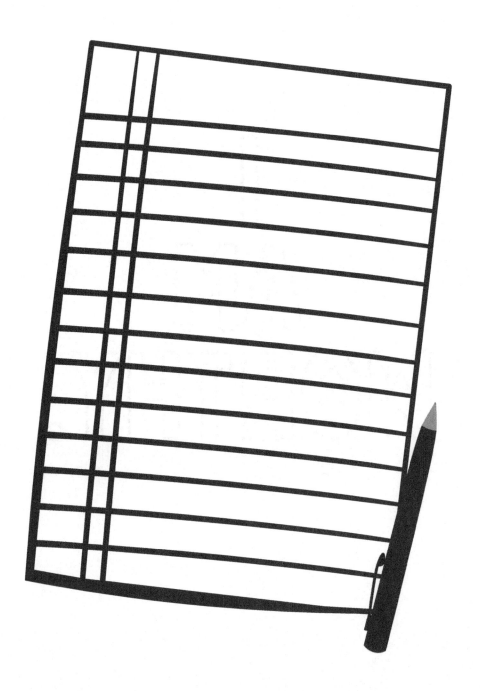

I LIKE MYSELF THE WAY I AM.

Life doesn't get easier, but we get stronger! What are at least 3 of your strengths?

I ENJOY AND EMBRACE CHALLENGES.

Make someone smile with a little note of positivity. Send a text to cheer someone up.

I SHOW EMPATHY.

Everyone needs a safe place. Where do you feel safe and comfortable?

I AM SAFE.

Take deep breaths, stress less, and practice daily mindfulness. Color and take a mindful moment.

I AM CREATIVE.

Difficulties are opportunities to grow.
What was a difficult time?
How did you overcome it?

I
HAVE
PERSISTANCE.

Breathing is the best way to calm our bodies and minds. Practice controlling your breath with box breathing.
Use your finger to trace.

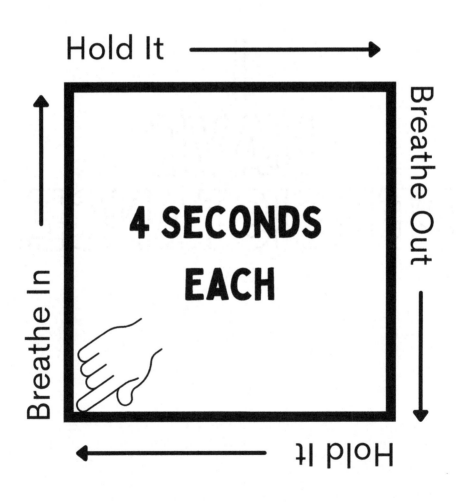

Hold It ⟶

Breathe Out

Breathe In

4 SECONDS EACH

Hold It ⟵

I FORGIVE MY MISTAKES.

Play hard and have fun!
How can you add fun to your day?

I AM THE BEST.

What is a song that makes you happy?

Now Playing:

I AM CREATIVE.

You have to love yourself first.
How can I show myself more love?

I LOVE ALL OF ME.

Books create magic and spread positivity. What book makes you happy?

I AM MAGICAL.

Never stop growing. Never stop learning. What is something that you learned recently?

I AM SMART.

Strive for progress over perfection. What are at least 3 things I can improve in?

I STRIVE FOR PROGRESS, NOT PERFECTION.

You are AMAZING!
Make a list of positive statements about you!

------------------------------- *I am enough*

I BELIEVE IN MYSELF.

Made in the USA
Middletown, DE
30 April 2022